SandCastle™
Let's Measure More

WHAT
IN THE
WORLD
IS A
BAKER'S
DOZEN?

AND OTHER
INTERESTING
MEASUREMENTS

A Division of ABDO

ABDO
Publishing Company

Desirée Bussiere

Consulting Editor, Diane Craig, M.A./Reading Specialist

visit us at www.abdopublishing.com

Published by ABDO Publishing Company, a division of ABDO, P.O. Box 398166, Minneapolis, Minnesota 55439. Copyright © 2013 by Abdo Consulting Group, Inc. International copyrights reserved in all countries. No part of this book may be reproduced in any form without written permission from the publisher. SandCastle™ is a trademark and logo of ABDO Publishing Company.

Printed in the United States of America, North Mankato, Minnesota
102012
012013

 PRINTED ON RECYCLED PAPER

Editor: Liz Salzmann
Content Developer: Nancy Tuminelly
Cover and Interior Design: Colleen Dolphin, Mighty Media, Inc.
Cover and Interior Production: Kate Hartman
Photo Credits: Shutterstock

Library of Congress Cataloging-in-Publication Data

Bussierre, Desireé, 1989- author.
 What in the world is a baker's dozen? : and other interesting measurements / Desireé Bussierre ; consulting editor, Diane Craig, M.A./reading specialist.
     pages cm. -- (Let's measure more)
Audience: 4-9
 ISBN 978-1-61783-595-7
1. Measurement--Juvenile literature. 2. Units of measurement--Juvenile literature. I. Title.
 QA465.B8978 2013
 530.8'1--dc23

                        2012024986

SandCastle™ Level: Transitional

SandCastle™ books are created by a team of professional educators, reading specialists, and content developers around five essential components—phonemic awareness, phonics, vocabulary, text comprehension, and fluency—to assist young readers as they develop reading skills and strategies and increase their general knowledge. All books are written, reviewed, and leveled for guided reading, early reading intervention, and Accelerated Reader® programs for use in shared, guided, and independent reading and writing activities to support a balanced approach to literacy instruction. The SandCastle™ series has four levels that correspond to early literacy development. The levels are provided to help teachers and parents select appropriate books for young readers.

| Emerging Readers (no flags) | Beginning Readers (1 flag) | Transitional Readers (2 flags) | Fluent Readers (3 flags) |

Contents

What do we

We measure everything! There are many interesting ways to measure.

measure?

A dozen is a group of twelve. A baker's dozen is one extra. It equals 13.

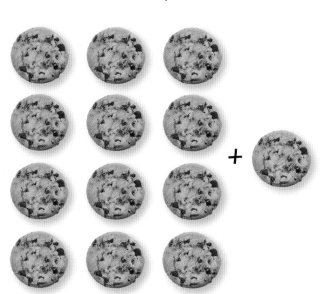

baker's dozen?

Jane helps out at a **bakery**. Joe loves cookies. He buys a dozen. Jane gives him a baker's dozen.

Twelve dozen is a gross.
One gross equals 144.

a gross?

Amelia's dad is a teacher. He orders a gross of pencils. The pencils are red.

Farmers use pecks and bushels. They measure fruits and vegetables.

A peck of apples is about 32 apples. There are four pecks in a bushel.

pecks & bushels?

Brandon picks apples. So do his parents and sister. They each pick a peck of apples. All together, they picked a bushel of apples.

A ream is used to measure paper. One ream is 500 sheets of paper.

a ream?

Jasmine puts one ream of paper in the printer. She prints her book report. She read a book about an eagle.

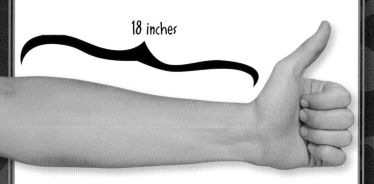

A cubit is used to measure length. It is very old.

The cubit is based on a person's **forearm**. It is about 18 inches (46 cm).

18 inches

a cubit?

Hunter studies ancient Egypt. The Egyptians built **pyramids**. They used cubits to measure the stones.

A watt is used to measure electric power. A 60-watt **lightbulb** uses 60 watts of electricity.

a watt?

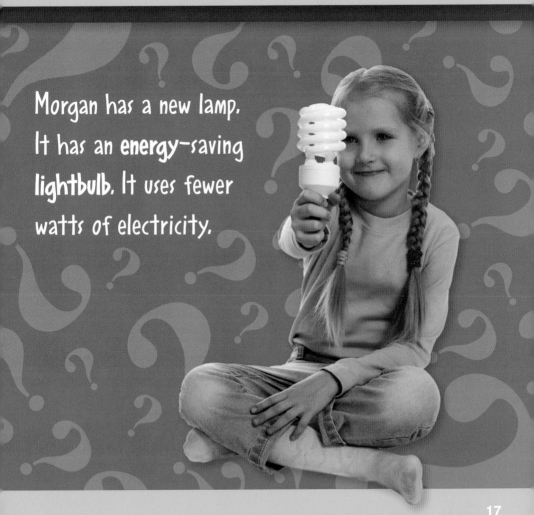

Morgan has a new lamp. It has an **energy-saving lightbulb**. It uses fewer watts of electricity.

Horsepower is used to measure engine power. It compares engines to horses.

Car, boat, and train engines are measured in horsepower.

horsepower?

Nate rides in his family's boat. It has a 50 horsepower engine. It goes very fast!

Degrees are used to measure **temperature.** There are two main temperature **scales.** They are Fahrenheit and Celsius.

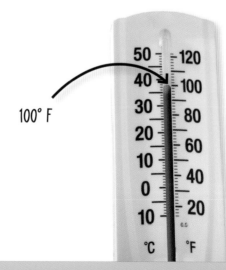

100° F

a degree?

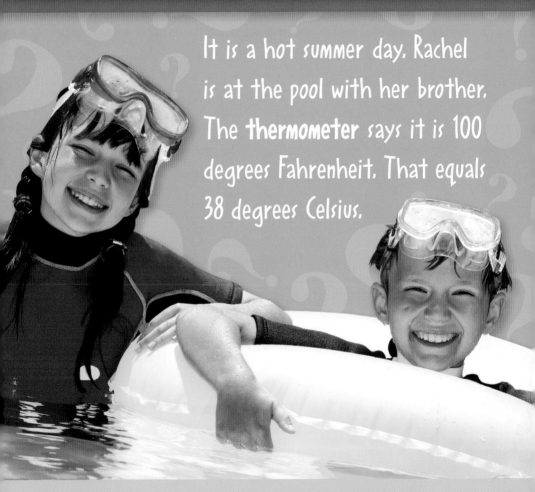

It is a hot summer day. Rachel is at the pool with her brother. The **thermometer** says it is 100 degrees Fahrenheit. That equals 38 degrees Celsius.

Fun facts

⇨ The oldest measurements used parts of the body. People measured with their arms, hands, fingers, and feet.

⇨ One bushel of apples can make 15 apple pies!

⇨ The watt is named after James Watt. He was a Scottish inventor.

⇨ People in the United States use degrees Fahrenheit. People in Europe use degrees Celsius.

Quiz

Read each sentence below. Then decide whether it is true or false.

1. A baker's dozen equals 13. True or False?

2. A peck is used to measure liquids. True or False?

3. One ream equals 500 sheets of paper.
   True or False?

4. A cubit is based on a person's leg. True or False?

5. There is more than one **temperature scale**.
   True or False?

Answers: 1. True   2. False   3. True   4. False   5. True

Glossary

bakery – a place where breads and pastries are made.

energy – power from sources such as oil and electricity that is used to run machines and heat buildings.

forearm – the part of the arm between the wrist and elbow.

lightbulb – the part of an electric lamp that glows and can be replaced.

pyramid – an Egyptian monument that is square on the bottom with four sides shaped like triangles.

scale – a system that uses a series of numbers, units, or values to measure something.

temperature – a measure of how hot or cold something is.

thermometer – a tool used to measure temperature.